50 Cheeky Truths to Improve Your Day

Or Year if You're a ~~Lazy~~ *Slow* Reader

By:

MATTHEW A. GALLAGHER

Copyright © 2019 Matthew A. Gallagher

All rights reserved.

Written, published, printed, and bound in THE UNITED STATES OF AMERICA.

Lorem ipsum dolor sit amet and whatever else is written onto blank websites.
Why are you reading this? It's a copyright page. Turn over to the next page and get to the good stuff.

Press, media, and general inquiry:
Email – info@50cheekytruths.com

Lawsuits and hate-mail:
Snail mail – 1600 Pennsylvania Ave. NW, Washington DC 20500

ISBN: 978-0-9988083-6-9 (paperback: English)
ISBN: 978-0-9988083-7-6 (paperback: Español)

Editing by Randy Peyser of Author One Stop, Inc.
Cover design by Peter and Caroline O'Connor

First printing April 2019.

Published by Matthew A. Gallagher
P.O. Box 836
Austin, Texas USA 78767

Acknowledgements

To Caroline and Peter of London, England – thank you for your incredible work on the cover designs.

To Fiverr – thank you for building a platform that connected me with some great graphic designers and artists who contributed to the artwork featured throughout this book.

Special thanks to artist *Vespavespo* for contributing a bulk of the artwork.

To my incredible colleagues from Facebook and Gartner – thank you for your support through my varied ambitions.

It's been great working with all of you, and I'm honored to call many of you lifelong friends.

Acknowledgements

To my buddies from LSU and back home from Shreveport – thank you for helping me develop my twisted sense of humor.

It is something I greatly appreciate, even if the majority of my Tinder and Bumble dates don't.

To my readers – thank you for reading my work and for buying a copy of this book.

Y'all are the real MVPs.

To Mama Gallagher – thank you for always providing guidance in times of need and encouragement when the odds weren't the best.

Time to reshuffle the deck.

Reactions and Rave Reviews

"The images, the setups, the punchlines – all HILARIOUS."

"50 Cheeky Truths is EXACTLY what I needed to read. Thank you for publishing this!"

"Purchased copies for my officemates. They loved it!"

"First time I have laughed this hard in a long time. Great work!"

"Improve your day? More like a week. The book was funny and wise from cover to cover!"

"Who reads these reviews anyway? But yeah, it's a solid read for $6... or whatever."

"Bark! Bark!" – Stray dog

Dedicated to Jesus and God

(Just in case)

Cheeky Truth I

The speed at which someone forgives you...

...is proportional to how much that individual likes you.

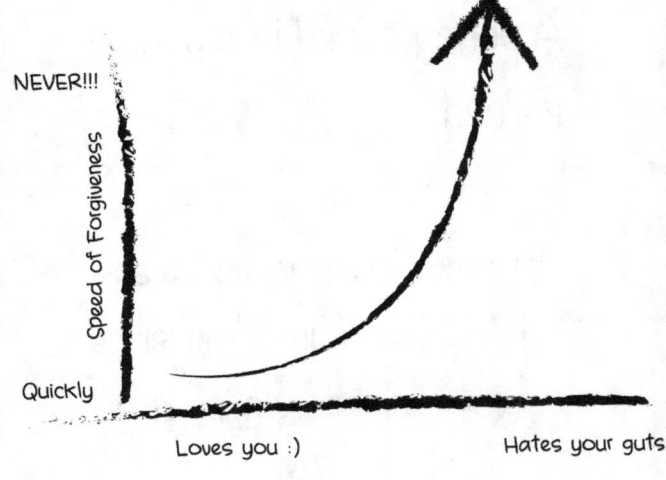

Cheeky Truth II

A penny saved is a penny earned...

But a federal minimum wage of $7.25 an hour will never be a livable wage.

(Step it up, Congress.)

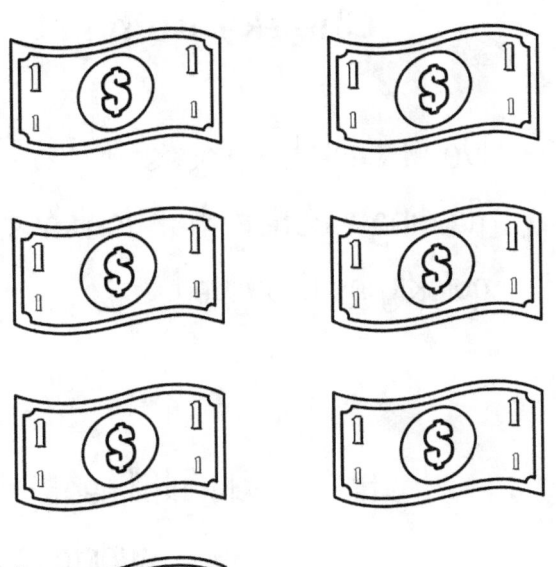

Cheeky Truth III

Don't seek happiness. It is a fleeting emotion that vanishes as quickly as it arrived.

Instead, seek fulfillment – it's worth more.

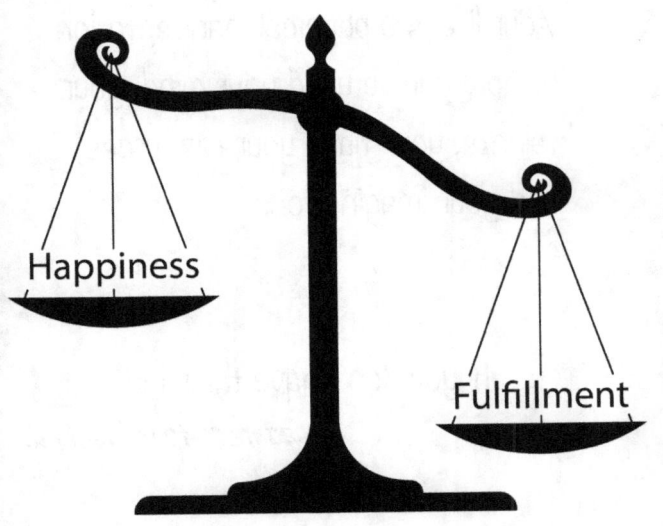

Cheeky Truth IV

Your life is a physical manifestation of how you've used your mind, your talents, your time, your resources, and your imagination.

If you don't have the mind...
read more to cultivate it.

If you don't have the talent...
practice your skills until you do.

If you don't have the time...
        reprioritize.

If you don't have the resources...
        acquire them.

If you don't know how to acquire them...
        borrow them.

If you don't have the imagination...

Micro-dose LSD.

(Everyone does it.)

17

Cheeky Truth V

You can do everything right – and still fail.

Take risks.

At the end of your life you're...

(insert whatever your religion makes you believe)

...anyway.

So what's the point of being afraid?

Cheeky Truth VI

Building wealth and staying fit are simple...

To build wealth, you must save more money than you spend and increase your income...

To stay fit, you must eat less calories than you burn and continue to exercise...

For some reason, most of us do the opposite.

Cheeky Truth VII

You have two ears for a reason...

Listen more.

(Good thing van Gogh isn't around anymore, or this one would have been awkward.)

Cheeky Truth VIII

There aren't many things you can buy that make you a richer person...

Except education, travel, and experiences...

...and really good sex, but that's illegal to purchase in most states.

✈ **ONE WAY FLIGHT**

LAS VEGAS
_____
_____
_____

Cheeky Truth IX

Spending too much money and eating unhealthy food is like masturbation...

It's fun and feels good to do...

But at the end of the day, you're just *f*#%ing* yourself.

Cheeky Truth X

There are no guarantees in life...

Except death and taxes.

And that Meryl Streep will win another Oscar.

She's just too damn talented.

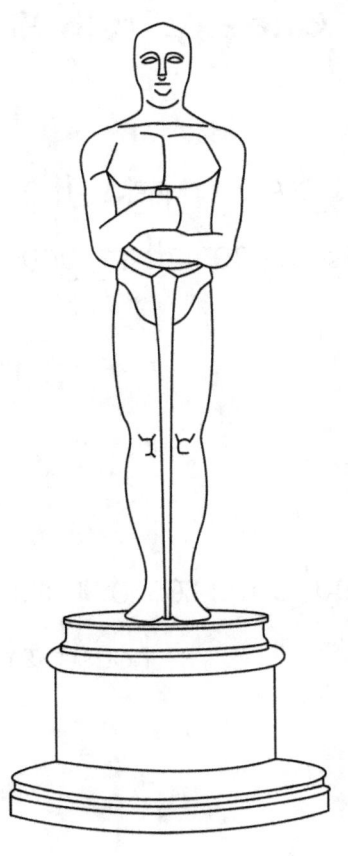

Cheeky Truth XI

If cats are ever jerks, it's because of something you did.

They're the real owners of the house, after all.

Cheeky Truth XII

Jack could have fit on the door...

But if the Titanic didn't sink, we wouldn't have the Federal Reserve today.

"Checkmate, Movie Lovers!"

- *Historians and Economists*

Cheeky Truth XIII

News entertainers aren't the experts they position themselves to be...

If they were, they'd work in the Private Sector or for the White House...

...and get paid *waaaay* more money.

Cheeky Truth XIV

Schrödinger's cat was just an elaborate prank.

The cat is fine.

Unless you turn this page over...

GREAT!
Look at what you did.

He's dead...

Way to go, champ.

You're a jerk for that. Poor little guy didn't deserve it.

#RIP

Cheeky Truth XV

If you have to leave your home for an extended period of time, like for a vacation or a natural disaster, leave a tall glass of frozen water (ice) in the freezer and place a quarter on top.

If you come back to a glass of ice and the quarter is not on the top, then your freezer thawed and items refroze. The food is ruined and should be considered unsafe to eat.
You should throw everything away and get new items.

This book just saved your life.
You're welcome.

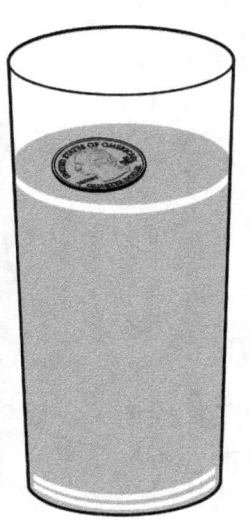

Cheeky Truth XVI

Just because some people are snarky, doesn't mean they can't be helpful.

Same goes for books.

Case in point...
that previous helpful tip
from Cheeky Truth XV.

Again, *this book saved your life.*

You're welcome.

Cheeky Truth XVII

You shouldn't care so much about your appearance and presence on social media...

You can't pay your bills in *'likes',* and vain comments won't keep you warm at night.

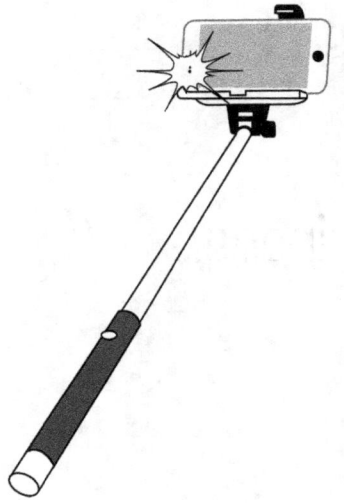

Cheeky Truth XVIII

Money
doesn't
buy
happiness...

...but it does buy you **freedom** and **whiskey**.

And that's pretty damn close.

Cheeky Truth XIX

There is no "I" in *team*..

...but there is an "I" in *dying alone*

Don't be a selfish prick and you won't.

Cheeky Truth XX

Never tease someone for the way they laugh, smile, or eat...

If you do, they'll never want to do any of those three things around you.

Cheeky Truth XXI

Laughter is the best medicine...

Unless you have chlamydia – then it's a few shots of penicillin...

...and better decision making on Friday nights.

Cheeky Truth XXII

If you use someone else's work while in school, it's considered "cheating" or "plagiarism"...
...and gets you expelled.

In the real world, it's called "resourcefulness" and "collaboration"...
...and gets you a raise.

Cheeky Truth XXIII

You learn more through failure than through success...

And you learn even more if you know how to use Google first.

How to not f#*% up

Cheeky Truth XXIV

Working hard isn't the key to success...

Being perceived as working hard is.

Unless you are a business owner.

In which case... put down the damn book and get back to building your empire.

You've got dreams to chase!

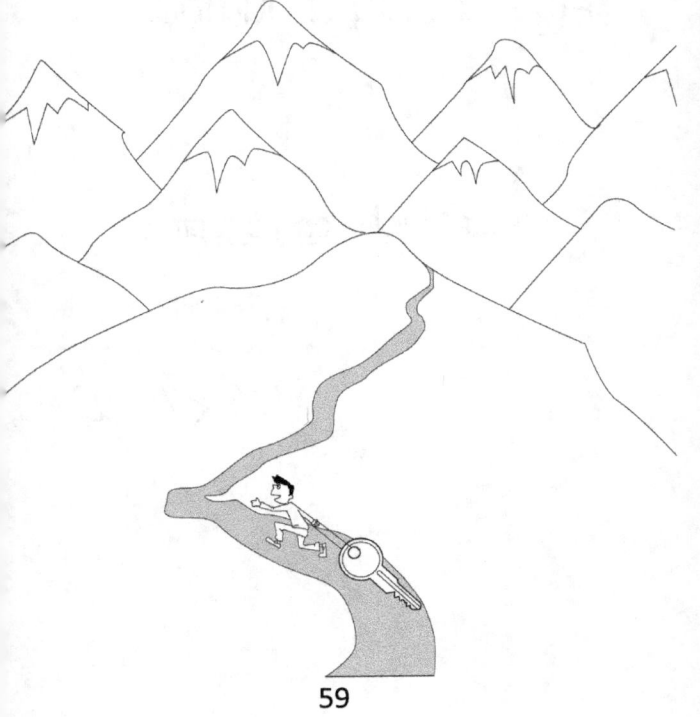

Cheeky Truth XXV

Age is only a number...

...and jail is only a room.

(Ask for I.D.)

Cheeky Truth XXVI

A person who is resourceful with little resources….

...is infinitely more effective than an apathetic person with an abundance of resources.

Cheeky Truth XXVII

Correlation does not always equal causation.

Reexamine the data and ask harder questions.

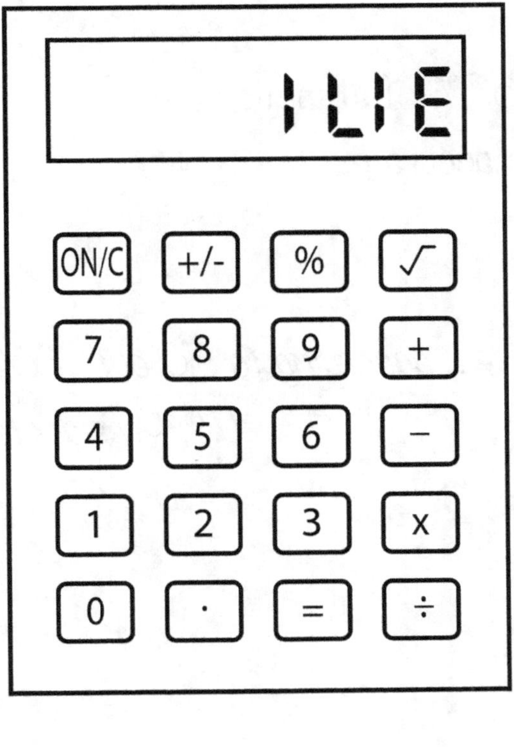
ILIE
ON/C
+/-
%
√
7
8
9
+
4
5
6
−
1
2
3
x
0
·
=
÷

Cheeky Truth XXVIII

63% of statistics are inaccurate...

...according to 50 out of 62 U.S. Presidents.

YAY

NAY

Cheeky Truth XXIX

Life is way too short to be weak with your words.

Speak **boldly.**

Cheeky Truth XXX

Ask for forgiveness, not for permission.

Better yet, just have a believable alibi and claim validation.

Plausible deniability mitigates most risks.

Cheeky Truth XXXI

Never say the phrase "touching base", when contacting someone...

It sounds creepier than you think.

Wait!

I just wanted to touch base

Cheeky Truth XXXII

All languages should be cherished for the richness they bring to global culture...

...except for corporate speak.

Don't believe me?

Next slide please –

Just circle back to this content after capturing that low-hanging fruit.

I'll ping you RE: this chapter and piggyback off of the previous point to double down on the core competencies.

It's in the T's and C's.

Regards,
-M

Cheeky Truth XXXIII

If you always long for the *"good old days"*....

...then you marginalize the present of its greatness...

...and strip the future of its potential.

Cheeky Truth XXXIV

This equation is more valuable than anything you learned in algebra.

$$H = \left(\frac{r}{e}\right) \cdot G^o$$

H = Happines
R = Reality
E = Expectation
G = Gratitude
O = Optimism

Cheeky Truth XXXV

You don't get what you deserve in life, you get what you negotiate.

Aim higher and allow yourself to negotiate down to a deal that still works for you.

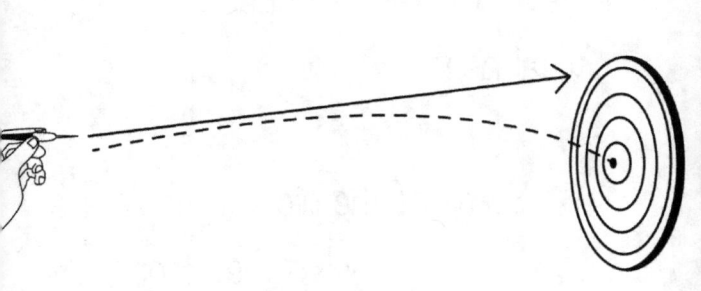

Cheeky Truth XXXVI

Never mistake kindness for weakness.

Some of the nicest people are also the strongest.

Cheeky Truth XXXVII

Don't compare yourself to others. Only compare yourself to the best version of you.

The true way to progress is to run your own race.

Or trip the other runners...
...whatever floats your boat.

Cheeky Truth XXXVIII

Focus on the breadth and depth of life...

...not only its length.

What's the point of aging to 100 if you never truly lived?

Cheeky Truth XXXIX

Some people die at 25...

...but aren't buried until they're 80.

Don't settle easily.

Cheeky Truth XL

Complacency leads to apathy.

Apathy leads to stagnation.

Stagnation leads to death.

Whether its life, love, or business – never become complacent.

Complacency

Apathy

Stagnation

Cheeky Truth XLI

Asking for help isn't a sign of <u>weakness</u>, it's a sign of *maturity*.

Know your limits
and be kind to yourself – ask for
help when needed.

Cheeky Truth XLII

Creativity creates.

The mind once stretched can never go back to its original limitations.

Cheeky Truth XLIII

The strongest destructive force known to man is fast moving bodies of water over long periods of time...

...followed by the second and third strongest destructive force – *apathy and speculation.*

Cheeky Truth XLIV

Exercise like a champion, and you'll sleep like a baby.

Work like a horse, and you'll eat like a king.

Read like a bookworm, and you'll miss all the great movies and shows your cooler friends always talk about.

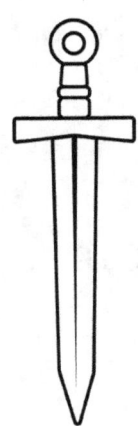

SICK REFERENCES ARE COMING

Cheeky Truth XLV

You can please some people all of the time.

You can please all people some of the time.

But you can never please all people all of the time.

Cheeky Truth XLVI

Some people want to get married...

Others want to *BE* married.

It is important to know the difference.

Cheeky Truth XLVII

Great relationships aren't built upon how happy the other person makes you...

...they are built upon how much happiness it gives you to make the other person happy, and vice versa.

Cheeky Truth XLVIII

<u>Good things</u> come to those who *wait.*

<u>Great things</u> come to those who *work.*

But <u>nothing</u> comes to those who *merely complain.*

Cheeky Truth XLIX

Team work makes the dream work!

Unless your team is full of people who wait for that <u>one</u> person who will do *all* the work.

Looking at you Sharon, Rob, and Tina.

Cheeky Truth L

One of the most important skills you can learn is how to bow out gracefully...

...whether it is in business,
in relationships,
or even in friendships.

Always exit with grace whenever possible.

And when it is *not* possible...

Go rogue!

Scorched earth mother*******!!!!

Cheeky Truth LI

WHAT IS THIS? A *bonus* Cheeky Truth?

My, my... what a lucky day for you, isn't it?

That said...

Always under-promise and over-deliver!

Get it?!...... FIN
Like *"The End"* in French...

but a <u>*shark* fin?</u>

HA!
No?

Alright, I'll see myself out...

Thank you for reading!

I hope that my work brought some laughter to your day and that you found the time reading well spent!

The purpose of this book was to bring simple joy to you, my cherished reader – because the world needs more positivity.

Whether it is an act of kindness, recognition of those around you, or even a quick laugh from a goofy book – it's on all of us to drive that positivity forward.

With that in mind, I hope you will consider donating to one of the wonderful organizations listed on the last two pages of this book.

Each one represents a cause that is important to bettering others and they are all dedicated to creating positive change for people around the world.

Thank you again for reading!

> Respectfully yours,
> *Matt*

P.S. If you liked the book and agree that the world needs more positivity, I hope you'll consider sharing your copy of *50 Cheeky Truths to Improve Your Day* with a friend or loved one.

P.P.S. Better yet – if you *loved* the book and believe it can bring positivity to those closest to you…

…then I hope you will consider buying and gifting copies of it to your friends, family, or your officemates. ☺

Then you will be able to watch the positivity spread to everyone near you.

Thanks again for reading!

Want to read Matthew's first book which is polar opposite to this one and way more important/informative?

Head over to Amazon.com and search for 'The Influence of Man'.
And, no, it isn't sexist. I promise.

List of Non-Profits

Black Girls Code –
www.BlackGirlsCode.com
A non-profit providing education within the field of technology to African American girls and other underrepresented groups in the tech industry. Having helped over 10,000 girls since their founding in 2011, Black Girls Code has a goal to provide education to over 1 million young women by 2040.

He For She –
www.HeForShe.org/en
A global initiative created by the United Nations for the advancement of gender equality worldwide. They encourage people to advocate for the improvement of circumstances and opportunities for everyone around them – no matter their gender.

Habitat for Humanity –
www.Habitat.org
An international organization dedicated to everyone in the world a decent place to live. Through building homes and renovating old houses, Habitat for Humanity has helped over 1 million families in need.

Operation Homefront –
www.OperationHomeFront.org
A national nonprofit whose mission is to provide financial assistance programs and other services for U.S. veterans and their families to gain stable housing.

World Wildlife Fund –
www.worldwildlife.org
An international non-governmental organization working around the world for wildlife preservation and the conservation of endangered species.

Now go forth and add!

I mean, *subtract!*

Or was it divide or multiply?

I can't remember…

…but whatever it is,
go for it!

www.ingramcontent.com/pod-product-compliance
Lightning Source LLC
Chambersburg PA
CBHW050437010526
44118CB00013B/1567